images of the
San Juan Islands

The Port of Friday Harbor, San Juan Island

images of the
San Juan Islands

Mark B. Gardner

Rainshadow Arts

Waiting for passengers to the San Juans, Anacortes, Washington

A ferry passes through Harney Channel, between Orcas and Shaw Islands

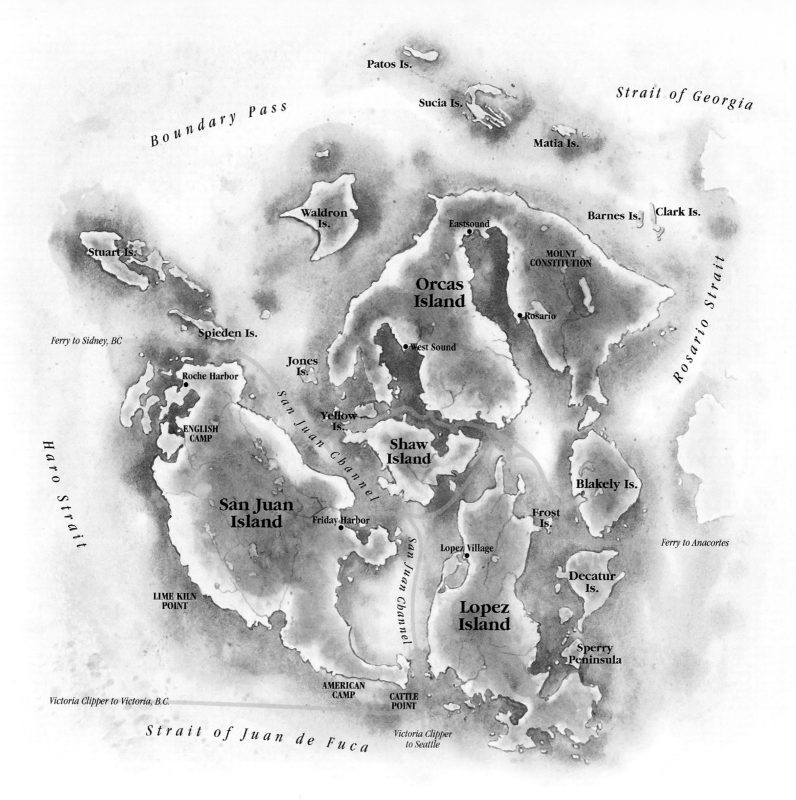

Patos Is.

Strait of Georgia

Boundary Pass

Sucia Is.

Matia Is.

Waldron Is.

Barnes Is. Clark Is.

Eastsound

Stuart Is.

MOUNT CONSTITUTION

Rosario Strait

Orcas Island

Spieden Is.

Rosario

Ferry to Sidney, BC

West Sound

Jones Is.

Roche Harbor

San Juan Channel

Yellow Is.

ENGLISH CAMP

Shaw Island

Haro Strait

Blakely Is.

Frost Is.

San Juan Island

Friday Harbor

San Juan Channel

Lopez Village

Ferry to Anacortes

Decatur Is.

LIME KILN POINT

Lopez Island

Sperry Peninsula

AMERICAN CAMP

CATTLE POINT

Victoria Clipper to Victoria, B.C.

Victoria Clipper to Seattle

Strait of Juan de Fuca

The morning fog lifts as the ferry enters the San Juan Islands through Thatcher Pass. Passengers on deck scan the waters ahead for an Orca's spout or simply bask in the emerging sunshine. The many islands seem to sparkle, dark green jewels against a bright blue sky. Even though I've traveled this route hundreds of times, I too become enthralled with the scenery and soon forget the book in front of me. A harbor seal surfaces near the ferry and watches us as intently as we watch him. Gulls soar just above the deck in the ferry's slipstream. Boats bob at anchor in the protected bays that we pass along the way. Commercial fishermen check their traps for tasty Dungeness Crabs. By the time the ferry lands, all on board are under the spell of the San Juan Islands.

Reachable only by boat or plane, this magic archipelago of 172 islands is tucked into the northwest corner of the United States. The Canadian border lies just a few miles to the north and to the west. Counting rocks with names, the number of islands rises to more than 400, some barely large enough to hold a basking seal. The San Juans are actually a small mountain chain created by uplift, then carved by glaciers, and now mostly submerged. The islands we see today are the tops of the chain's peaks and crags.

Surrounded by waters cooled year-round by Pacific currents and lying in the rain shadow of the Olympic Mountains, the San Juans enjoy a mild, often sunny, Mediterranean-type climate. Winter and spring are wet, but less so than on the mainland. The islands receive about half the annual rainfall of Seattle which is only 75 air miles away. Summer and fall are dry; more like those of California's central coast than the Pacific Northwest.

Their geologic youth, relatively dry climate and isolation makes the San Juans ecologically unique. The variety of habitats - from the marine waters surrounding the islands to the forested mountain slopes - creates a very diverse ecosystem. However, because the islands are isolated and relatively small, some species common on the nearby mainland, such as large predators, are absent here.

Open prairies dominate their southern flanks with tall grasses, wildflowers, and even prickly-pear cactus. Groves of Garry oak dot the same slopes giving some areas a savannah-like appearance. Species common in other regions but unusual on the northwest coast,

such as juniper and aspen grow throughout the islands. Perhaps the most distinctive tree is the Pacific madrona, which grows in tall, often beautifully sculpted twists and turns. Madronas keep their thick, waxy leaves in winter and shed their outer bark to reveal a bright red inner layer, which, in turn peals away in summer, exposing the soft, green wood beneath.

The islands' forests were heavily logged in the late 1800s and early 1900s to supply timber for shipbuilding and fuel for lime kilns. Today the islands have mostly recovered with a second-growth forest dominated by Douglas fir trees and an undergrowth of Oregon grape, salal, and wildflowers. There are still a few stands of old-growth with large western red cedar and Douglas fir trees. The forests on the islands' upper slopes also include grand fir, western hemlock, and other subalpine trees.

With their diversity of habitat, the San Juans are rich in bird life. Great blue herons, oystercatchers, and a variety of other shore birds live along the rocky shoreline. Trumpeter swans, Canada geese and a variety of waterfowl are common during winter. Birds of prey such as bald eagles and peregrine falcons

are relatively common. On the open water, you see diving birds such as the rhinoceros auklet, guillemots and endangered marbled murrelet.

Upland, feisty Anna's hummingbirds feed on the many wildflowers. Turkey vultures and harriers prowl above the prairies. Cooper's and sharp shinned hawks patrol the forests, where you often hear a Raven's "kronk" and a thrush's melodic song. The islands are also an important rest stop for birds migrating along the Pacific Flyway. Common murres, phalaropes, and other nonresident species are common visitors during spring and fall.

The waters surrounding the islands team with life. The Orca, or killer whale, is at the top of the marine food chain. The name "killer whale" is actually inappropriate as they are neither killers nor whales: Orcas have never been known to attack anything other than their usual prey, and they are actually the largest member of the dolphin family. About eighty-five whales in three pods are resident spring to fall. These whales are very social and hunt salmon cooperatively. During summer, the pods sometimes come together to form a "superpod" in which the males of one pod mate with the females of another. Each pod consists of related females and their young, accompanied by one or two unrelated bull males who are easily recognized by their size and towering dorsal fin. The whales are most active during the mating season and are often seen breaching and spyhopping, much to the delight of whale-watchers.

Nonresident Orca, called "transients", appear in the San Juans year round. Quite different from their cousins that live in pods, transients live alone or in small family groups of two to three whales. Rather than salmon, they hunt seals and other marine mammals. The whales that live in pods are very noisy, using sound to communicate. Transients, on the other hand, are very quiet; presumably so they don't alert their prey.

In addition to Orca, a variety of other marine mammals live in or travel through the islands' waters. Harbor seals, the most common, are frequently seen cruising in the water or resting on exposed rocks. One named "Popeye" hangs around the seafood dock in Friday Harbor and has trained the tourists to feed her. Sea lions, much larger than harbor seals, migrate through the islands to and from their breeding beaches in Alaska. Several minke whales live in the islands, and the odd gray whale shows up during migration. Dall's porpoises, resembling small killer whales feed in the eddylines of open water, and sometimes play in the bow wake of boats. River otters and mink live along the shoreline and forage for crabs and shellfish in shallow water.

Below the surface, an amazing menagerie of creatures attracts divers from around the world. The giant octopus is the most famous, but there are others that often defy the imagination, including many-armed starfish two feet in diameter, big white anemones that look like cauliflower heads atop tall stalks, and the wizened wolf-eel that grows to over ten feet long and eats urchins. The marine plant life is equally amazing. Beds of bull kelp dot the waters, growing from rocky bottom to the surface. Stands of eelgrass form a tall prairie on sandy bottoms, creating important nurseries for juvenile fish, including salmon.

Seeing most of this marine life requires at least a wet suit and snorkeling gear. However, some of these unusual creatures are revealed at low tide, where viewing them requires nothing more than a pair of tall rubber boots. Pasted on the exposed rocks, purple starfish, limpets, barnacles, and other species await the water's return. Tide pools resemble aquariums filled with small crabs, green sea anemones, pink coralline algae, and other curiosities. And the patches of crab-clawed rockweed are full of tiny crabs and colorful shellfish.

Humans have been part of the ecosystem for at least 9,000 years. Tribes of the southern Coast Salish lived in the San Juans for centuries prior to the arrival of Europeans. The Lummis, the predominant tribe, shared the islands with the Samish, Saanich, and Songish tribes. Archaeologists have found evidence of more than 280 settlements on San Juan Island alone, including a massive longhouse nearly 600 feet in length on the shore of Garrison Bay on San Juan Island.

These early inhabitants caught salmon in the open water, gathered shellfish in the intertidal zone, and foraged in the uplands. Facilitated by a common language and large canoes, the Salish tribes also traded extensively among themselves which led to a relatively peaceful culture. Other tribes, such as the Kwakuitl and Haida, visited the islands to trade with, and sometimes raid, the resident Salish.

Europeans finally came to the islands in 1791 when a boat from the Spanish expedition led by Francisco Eliza circled the archipelago. Eliza named the archipelago after the Viceroy of Mexico. The next year, the Spanish returned to explore further and unexpectedly encountered a larger British expedition led by George Vancouver. The Spanish accepted Vancouver's offer to collaborate on charting the area. The legacy of this collaboration remains in the Spanish names of many of the archipelago's islands and channels, including San Juan, Orcas, Lopez, Haro, and Rosario. Faced with bigger threats elsewhere, the Spanish abandoned the area soon after, leaving it to the British who claimed the entire region as part of their empire.

In 1846, the 49th parallel was established as the boundary between the expanding United States and British Territory. Unfortunately, the wording of the treaty left the ownership of the San Juan Islands in doubt. The British regarded Rosario Strait, east of the San Juans, as the boundary and thus claimed ownership of the archipelago. The Americans, however, regarded Haro Strait, as the boundary and also claimed the islands. Thus an otherwise insignificant cluster of islands became the stage for a clash between the aging British Empire and its upstart offspring.

Using their well-established position at Fort Victoria on Vancouver Island, the British gained control in the early 1850s by chartering the Hudson's Bay Company to colonize the islands. The Company built a significant farming and fishing operation under the protective shield of the British Navy. Meanwhile, the American government sent an expedition to map the area, and a handful of American settlers staked claims to the land used by the Hudson's Bay Company. Both sides expanded their presence throughout the 1850s, regarding each other as illegal squatters and periodically threatening each other with force. Except for a few minor skirmishes, neither side had the firepower or willpower to actually confront the other.

Tensions peaked in 1859 in what has become known as the Pig War, the last armed conflict between the United States and Britain. Fortunately, the only casualty was a Hudson's Bay Company pig who rooted in Lyman Cutler's potato patch one time too many. To protect the lives and property of their citizens, both nations sent in more military firepower, with the two sides facing off near Cattle Point on

San Juan Island. The American forces were under the command of then Lieutenant George Pickett of Civil War fame.

Fortunately cooler heads prevailed, and a crisis was averted. Both sides agreed to joint occupation until the dispute could be resolved. Finally, in 1872, Kaiser Wilhelm of Germany settled the argument in favor of the United States, setting the boundary through Boundary Pass and Haro Strait. Today, the legacy of the Pig War lives on at American Camp and English Camp, part of the San Juan Island National Historic Park.

Out of the spotlight of international conflict, the San Juans returned to being a rural backwater in a remote corner of the nation. For the next hundred years, the islands attracted little attention and the small population grew slowly. Islanders made their living by fishing, farming, building boats, logging and producing lime. Smuggling also has a long tradition in the San Juans. Through the years, colorful and sometimes ruthless characters like "Pig Iron" Kelly have smuggled Chinese railroad workers, Canadian wool, booze during Prohibition, and drugs more recently.

The boat building, large scale logging, and lime works are now long gone. Commercial fishermen continue to take salmon, but far fewer than the millions caught in the late 1800s and early 1900s. Today most commercial boats catch Dungeness crab, prawns, sea cucumber, and sea urchin. The occasional smuggler still slips across the border with illegal drugs, immigrants, and even Cuban cigars. Farming is still a big part of island life, defining much of the rural character of the islands.

Today, people come to the San Juans from all over the world to escape the mainland's pressures and enjoy the islands' slow pace, scenery, and outdoor recreation. The islands' Orca, natural beauty and protected waters are among the main attractions, but there are also sophisticated art galleries, quaint B&Bs, scenic bike rides, bustling farmers' markets, and award winning wineries. Some visitors stay only a few days, but an increasing number return frequently or simply never leave. Most people come to San Juan, Orcas, Lopez and Shaw, the largest islands and the only ones served by the Washington state ferries. Some of the smaller islands can be visited by water taxi or private boat, but most are privately owned or protected as preserves.

San Juan is the most populous and second largest of the islands. The archipelago's only incorporated town and its county seat, Friday Harbor, is located on the east side on a well-protected harbor of the same name. The town is a popular tourist destination and a bustling community with plenty of good restaurants, hotels, art galleries, gift shops, and the islands' only brew pub. The harbor has a working port where most of the islands' whale-watching fleet docks and commercial fishermen bring their catches.

Outside of town, San Juan Island is a rural patchwork of open prairie, farms, second growth forest, and residences. The island's southern end is largely open, rolling prairie that hosts colorful wildflowers in spring then turns golden brown in the dry summers. You often can see fox, which only live on San Juan Island, rabbits

descended from those raised by early settlers, deer as well as bald eagles and a variety of other birds. Further north, San Juan Island becomes more hilly and forested. Inland there are numerous farms that raise produce and hay as well as cattle, horses, llamas and their cute cousins, alpacas. You will also find a colorful lavender farm as well as an award-winning winery. There are several lakes that provide excellent bass

and trout fishing. Lime Kiln Point, on the island's west side, is the site of an old lighthouse and the country's only whale-watching park. During the summer, Orca often thrill visitors by swimming just off the rocky shore of the park and the public land just to the south. Roche Harbor, on the northern end, is a well-protected harbor with marina and historic resort.

Orcas Island is the largest of the San Juan Islands, but second most populated. It is a heavily wooded, almost mountainous, horseshoe-shaped island. Mount Constitution and the lesser peaks in Moran State Park fill the eastern side of the horseshoe. The road to the top of Mount Constitution winds through the forest, with occasional viewpoints, to a lookout with a magnificent view at the top. The Park has miles of hiking trails, several pristine lakes, relaxing campgrounds, and even cascading waterfalls. The eastern side of the horseshoe is also home to historic Rosario Resort, the old village of Olga, and always fun Doe Bay.

The village of Eastsound, the island's business center and home to a handful of shops, inns, and restaurants sits at the head of East Sound, at the apex of the horseshoe. On the horseshoe's west side, the rounded bulge of aptly named Turtleback Mountain looms over the pastures and orchards of Crow Valley as well as the bays of West Sound and Deer Harbor. Turtleback Mountain is now protected as a preserve with sweeping views of the archipelago. Deer Harbor hosts a busy marina, resort and activity center.

Lopez is the third largest island and third most populated. In contrast to Orcas's mountains, Lopez has open, gently rolling terrain, making it a popular destination for bicyclists. Lopez Village and nearby Fisherman Bay serve as the island's commercial center, with the rest of the island a patchwork of second-growth forests and working farms that produce cattle, sheep, truck crops, and even grapes for the island's excellent winery. Lopezians pride themselves on being the friendliest of the San Juan Islands and make a habit of waving to everyone they pass.

Lopez's puzzle-piece shape results from the islands' many tombolos, narrow spits formed by sediment deposited between two islands. Fisherman Bay and the Sperry Peninsula were formed by tombolos that connected Lopez to former islands. Spencer Spit is a tombolo that reaches for Frost Island, but a strong current keeps them from touching.

Shaw Island is the smallest of the ferry served islands. A heavily wooded island surrounded by its three bigger siblings, Shaw is best known for its solitude. Two orders of nuns, an order of monks, and a few hundred other people make

Shaw their home. With no restaurants or lodgings on the island, the island receives few visitors. Blind Bay, on the north side is one of the San Juan's best anchorages, and the county park on the south side has an excellent campground and beach.

None of the other islands are served by the ferry system, yet people live on many of them. Most have little public access and few amenities for visitors.

A few hundred self-sufficient residents determined to preserve the last island frontier live on Waldron, northwest of Orcas. They try to live as islanders did a century ago, growing or making what they need, and even have a one-room schoolhouse. Northeast of San Juan Island, Spieden Island is home to a few people and a large herd of exotic animals left over from its days as "Safari Island". The then owners stocked the island with "game animals" from Africa and Asia, and marketed safaris to well-heeled hunters. The operation went bust after a few years and left many of the animals behind.

Nearby Stuart Island, with a number of permanent and seasonal residents, is bisected by a state park and is a popular boating destination. Walking the county road takes you to an old lighthouse on the north end. Along the way, you pass the island's schoolhouse, where islanders keep a water cooler with paper cups for people and a dish for dogs. Canoe Island, between Shaw and Lopez, is host to a French Camp in the summer and is available for retreats and meetings.

A number of other islands are state parks accessible only by boat or float plane. Matia, Sucia, and Patos Islands line the northeastern corner of the archipelago.

Their yellowish rock, not found elsewhere in the San Juans, has been sculpted by wave action into sometimes surprising shapes. An old lighthouse on the northern tip of Patos stands watch over the archipelago's junction with the Strait of Georgia. Jones Island, another state park between Orcas and San Juan, is home to several nearly-tame deer which are always a big hit with visiting kids. Turn Island, just east of San Juan, often hosts a nesting pair of bald eagles and has excellent camping. And James Island greets ferry passengers on their voyage from Anacortes through Thatcher Pass. Many of these islands are part of the Cascadia Marine Trail, with campsites reserved for kayakers.

The remaining islands are either publicly or privately owned with little or no development or public access. Most are protected as preserves or as part of the San Juan Island National Wildlife Refuge. People are required to stay at least a hundred yards away to avoid disturbing the wildlife. Yellow Island, a preserve owned by the Nature Conservancy, is one of the few that individuals or small groups can visit. Each spring, wildflowers turn the island into a showy palette of colors, usually peaking around Mother's Day.

The San Juan Islands are a very special place, but one in danger of being loved to death. Currently, the San Juans are experiencing a resurgence of growth and popularity. Some islanders refer to this as a renaissance; others aren't so sure. But for good or bad, the influx of tourists, retirees, and seasonal residents is changing the islands, potentially threatening an environment and way of life that makes the islands special. Hopefully, the San Juan Islands will still be a magic place for the next generation of residents and visitors.

Mt. Rainier rises above Puget Sound
at dawn, from San Juan Island

13

Entering the San Juan Islands
through Thatcher Pass

Canoes from the Lummi Nation and Swinomish Indian
Tribal Community approach Shaw Island

The Adventuress at anchor, Prevost Harbor, Stuart Island

A ferry entering Friday Harbor

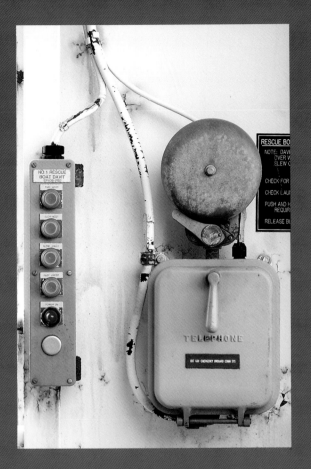

On the deck of the ferry,
Evergreen State

Poppies blooming in the
prairie at Cattle Point,
San Juan Island

Black-tailed deer, common
throughout the Islands

Lime Kiln Lighthouse,
San Juan Island

Inside Lime Kiln Lighthouse

False Bay at low tide, San Juan Island

South Beach, San Juan Island
National Historical Park,
San Juan Island

A boy and his best friend,
South Beach, San Juan Island

A Yellow Lab plays fetch at one
of the Islands' many beaches

English Camp, San Juan Island National Historical Park, San Juan Island

Fog shrouds Cattle Point at dawn, San Juan Island

Cattle Point from the east, San Juan Island

Fog fills San Juan
Valley on a late
summer morning,
San Juan Island

Winter sunset,
San Juan Island

Boat reflections

Restored wooden boats at Roche Harbor, San Juan Island

Historic Roche Harbor, San Juan Island

Friday Harbor with Griffin Bay beyond, San Juan Island

A ferry entering Friday Harbor, San Juan Island

Golden reflections on blue water

Sunset, Lime Kiln Point,
San Juan Island

Westcott Bay Institute Sculpture
Park at Roche Harbor,
San Juan Island

A kayak provides an intimate
view of a surfacing Orca

An old barn and older Garry Oak,
San Juan Island

Spring wildflowers in full bloom at American Camp,
San Juan Island National Historical Park, San Juan Island

Officers' Quarters, American Camp,
San Juan Island National Historical Park

A male California quail in
full breeding plumage

The flowering prairie at American Camp,
San Juan Island National Historical Park

A fox plays with one of her young kits

A fox kit lurks in the tall grass

A fox kit nuzzles his father

A yacht decorated for the annual
Christmas boat parade in Friday Harbor

Restored wooden sailing vessel
moored at Friday Harbor

The start of the Shaw Island Classic in San Juan Channel
between Shaw and San Juan Islands

Flying spinnaker, San Juan Channel

Enjoying a social paddle

Cycling through American Camp,
San Juan Island

The 4th of July parade in Friday Harbor

Islanders participating in the
4th of July parade in Friday Harbor

Fireworks, part of Friday Harbor's
4th of July celebration

Red sky at night, sailors delight,
San Juan Island

The Wasp Islands and Orcas Island

Old sign, West Beach,
Orcas Island

Deer Harbor, Orcas Island

Biking on the trails of Moran State Park, Orcas Island

Hiking in the old growth forest of
Moran State Park, Orcas Island

Cascade Falls, Moran State Park, Orcas Island

A summer morning at Orcas Village, Orcas Island

A winter morning at Orcas Village, Orcas Island

Lichens cover much of the
rock outcroppings in the San Juans

Spring ground cover of
blue-eyed mary and stonecrop

The view from
Turtleback Mountain,
Orcas Island

Sheep grazing in Crow Valley, Orcas Island

Curious calf, oblivious cows in one of the San Juan Islands' many herds

A lone horse enjoys the tall grass in his pasture

Cyclists disembark the ferry for the annual Tour de Lopez on Lopez Island

Kayaking at Iceberg Point, Lopez Island

Aerial view of Fisherman Bay on Lopez Island with Blakely, Decatur and Cyprus Islands beyond

Forest at the Shark Reef Recreation Area on Lopez Island

Bulrushes emerge from one of the many lakes that dot the San Juans

A pair of overwintering trumpeter swans enjoy a sunny day

Early morning mist rises as swallows swoop over Hummel Lake, Lopez Island

Steller sea lions on Bird Rocks in Rosario Strait

Pelagic cormorant

Harlequin ducks

Glaucous-winged and Heermann's gulls feed on a herring ball

A foraging river otter

Pigeon guillemot, which breed on
rocky bluffs throughout the Islands

Rhinoceros auklet, often seen feeding
in open waters between islands

Kelp bed and harbor seals,
Whale Rocks, San Juan Channel

Kids exploring a tide pool,
San Juan Island

Ochre sea stars revealed by low tide

Black oystercatchers probe the
rockweed for food at low tide

Small sea anemones cover the
bottom of a tide pool

Ochre sea stars and bull kelp

Surfing Orca

Spyhop

Surfacing bull Orca

The lighthouse at Turn Point on Stuart Island marks the northwest corner of the San Juan archipelago

Large boulders left by glaciers line the beach on Clark Island; Little Sister and Orcas Islands lie beyond

Camas and chocolate lilies, Yellow Island

A colorful palette of spring wildflowers, including
paintbrush, camas and buttercup, Yellow Island

A flower-filled knoll overlooks the caretaker's cabin on Yellow Island,
a preserve owned by the Nature Conservancy

Shell fragments, the beach at
English Camp, San Juan Island

Sandstone pattern,
Sucia Island

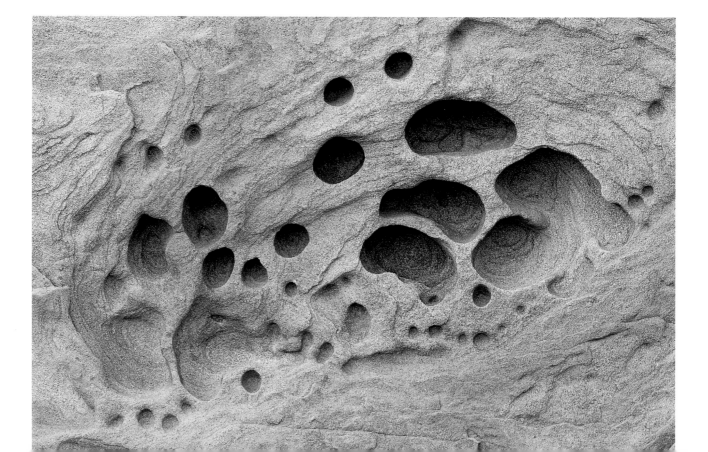

A golden wave of sculpted sandstone, Cluster Islets near Sucia Island

Lighthouse, Alden Point, Patos Island and Mt. Baker

Boats at anchor on a quite summer evening, Reid Harbor, Stuart Island

The colorful Pacific madrona grows
throughout the San Juans

Pacific tree frog

Peeling bark of the Pacific madrona

A bald eagle surveys her domain from the top of a Douglas fir tree

An immature bald eagle
flexes its wings

A bald eagle sits in
one of the many nests
found in the San Juans

Bald eagle about to take flight

Fawn lily,
another
early spring
wildflower

Shooting stars are one of the earliest
wildflowers to emerge in the spring

Fairyslipper, a showy orchid found on
the forest floor throughout the islands

Lavender fields, Pelindaba Lavender Farm, San Juan Island

Hay bales dot one of the many pastures on San Juan Island

Raking hay the old fashioned way, Heritage Farm, San Juan Island

A large crowd shops at
the farmers' market,
San Juan Island

Vignettes from the
farmers' market,
San Juan Island

Delicious Dungeness
crabs wait for buyers

Crab boat, Friday Harbor,
San Juan Island

Old crab pot floats and an oar

Crab pots, ready for fishing

A tugboat guards a tanker laden with Alaskan Oil, Rosario Strait

A rainbow touches down
on Lopez Island

A ferry disappears into the summer fog, bound for Anacortes

Heading home from a summer cruise

Ferry docking at the terminal in Anacortes, Washington

Sunset over Stuart and Johns Islands, with the Canadian Gulf Islands beyond

ACKNOWLEDGMENTS

As with any project like this, many people helped along the way. I especially thank Alston Gardner and Barb Lee, without whom this project would not have been possible. I also thank Alan and Katy Barsamian, Larry Marx, Roger and Michelle Shober, Bill and Colleen Wright of San Juan Safaris, Ruth Offen of waterworks gallery, Pat Lawrence, Claudia Fullerton of Island Studios, Deb McEdward, Pat and Lanny Carver, Dane Armstrong of Friday Harbor Helicopters, Alice Acheson, Laura Norris of Griffin Bay Bookstore, Joe & Sally Todd, Jim Rabenhorst, Claudia La Cava and Mike Macdonald of At Home Magazine, and the many other islanders who provided ideas, encouragement and assistance; Bob Hale and Oscar Lind of Robert Hale & Company for help in publishing; Rick Alton for turning digital files into this book; Gary Hawkey and the team at iocolor, my son, Ben, for helping me in lots of ways; and finally my wife, Dona Reed, whose help and support made my life, this book and my images far better than they otherwise would have been.

DEDICATION

This book is dedicated to the memory of Susan Eyerly and Larry McEdward who loved these islands more than any other place.

Printed in China
Published by Rainshadow Arts, Inc.

Cover photograph: Before dawn, south end of San Juan and Lopez Islands
Cover and interior photographs: Mark B. Gardner

Cover Design: Rick Alton, Alton Media
Interior design and composition: Rick Alton, Alton Media
Library of Congress Cataloging-in-Publication Data is available
ISBN-13: 978-0-9753068-1-9
ISBN-10: 0-9753068-1-2

Rainshadow Arts, Inc.   360-378-1371
144 Panorama Place   www.imagesofthesanjuans.com
Friday Harbor, WA 98250   info@imagesofthesanjuans.com

Western bluebirds, one of the pair released by the San Juan Islands Western Bluebird Reintroduction Project